NEW SERIES!
Good for Me

Reading Level: Grades 1-2
Interest Level: Grades K-3
By featuring tips about healthy snacks and meals, this series provides children with a chance to develop a positive outlook on maintaining a balanced diet.
Publisher: Rosen Publishing (PowerKids Press)
Discount: Prices reflect 25% off list
Binding: Reinforced Library
Size: 8 x 9 • Pages: 24
Features: Full-Color Photographs, Websites, Glossary, Index

____	**RPK505**	**GOOD FOR ME (6 vols.)**	**95.70**
____	RP2678	Fruit/Hewitt, Spr 08	15.95
____	RP2708	Grains and Cereals/Hewitt, Spr 08	15.95
____	RP2661	Meat and Fish/Hewitt, Spr 08	15.95
____	RP2685	Milk and Cheese/Hewitt, Spr 08	15.95
____	RP2654	Vegatables/Hewitt, Spr 08	15.95
____	RP2913	Water/Hewitt, Spr 08	15.95

Good For Me
Fruit

Sally Hewitt

PowerKiDS
press.

New York

Notes for Teachers and Parents

Good for Me is a series of books that looks at ways of helping children to develop a positive approach to eating. You can use the books to help children make healthy choices about what they eat and drink as an important part of a healthy lifestyle.

Look for fruit when you go shopping.
- Look at the different types of fruit in your local supermarket.
- Read the ingredients on packages to see if the food contains fruit.
- Buy something new. Have fun preparing it and eating it with children.

Talk about different food groups and how we need to eat a variety of foods from each group every day.
- Fruit is packed with vitamins, minerals, and fiber.
- Talk about the ways vitamins, minerals, and fiber help to keep us strong and healthy.

Talk about how we feel when we are healthy and the things we can do to help us to stay healthy.
- Eat food that is good for us.
- Drink plenty of water.
- Enjoy fresh air and exercise.
- Sleep well.

Published in 2008 by The Rosen Publishing Group, Inc.
29 East 21st Street, New York, NY 10010

Copyright © 2008 Wayland/The Rosen Publishing Group, Inc.

First Edition

Produced by Tall Tree Ltd.
Editor: Jon Richards
Designer: Ben Ruocco
Consultant: Sally Peters

Library of Congress Cataloging-in-Publication Data

Hewitt, Sally, 1949—
   Fruit / Sally Hewitt. — 1st ed.
     p. cm. — (Good for me)
   Includes index.
   ISBN 978-1-4042-4267-8 (library binding)
   1. Fruit—Juvenile literature. 2. Cookery (Fruit)—Juvenile literature. I. Title.
   TX397.H49 2008
   641.3'5—dc22
                              2007032508

Manufactured in China

Contents

Good for me

Everyone needs to eat food and drink water to live, grow, and be **healthy**. All the food we eat comes from animals and plants. Fruit is food from plants.

Fruit comes in all different shapes, sizes, and colors, including green apples and red cherries.

You can pick your
own fruit, such as
strawberries, at
local farms.

Fruit is grown in **orchards**, on farms,
and in gardens. It needs rain and
sunshine to grow and become **ripe**.
This means that the fruit is ready to eat.

Vitamins, minerals, and fiber

Fruit is full of **vitamins** and **minerals**. Every part of your body needs vitamins and minerals to be healthy and to fight **germs**.

Eating crunchy fruit helps to keep your teeth strong and healthy.

Fruit contains natural sugar that gives you **energy**. It is also full of **fiber** that helps your body to get rid of unwanted food.

Oranges contain lots of vitamin C, which can help to stop you from catching colds.

Lunchbox

Squeeze fresh oranges for a healthy drink at lunchtime.

Fruit from trees

Many trees produce fruit in order to protect their **seeds**, including apples, cherries, and pears. We grow fruit trees in farms called orchards.

Cherry trees grow flowers, called blossoms, before they grow fruit.

Pears and apples contain seeds inside them, which are surrounded by the hard fruit.

Fruit is juicy because it stores food for a plant's seeds. When the fruit falls from a tree, the seed inside starts to grow. The fruit gives the seed the food it needs to grow.

Lunchbox

Combine some chopped apples, chopped celery, walnuts, raisins, and mayonnaise to make a Waldorf salad.

All over the world

Fruit is sent all over the world inside trucks, boats, and planes. These vehicles have special fridges and freezers that keep the fruit fresh. This means that you can eat fruit that has traveled thousands of miles.

This pink, spiky fruit is called rambutan. It comes from Thailand.

You can eat bananas that have come from Africa, pineapples from the Philippines, and kiwi fruit that has come from New Zealand.

Bananas are green and unripe when they are packed and shipped. The bananas turn yellow when they are ripe.

Lunchbox

Make a fruit salad from all over the country: use Florida mangoes, New Jersey blueberries, and Californian oranges.

Growing fruit

Fruit grows on plants of all shapes and sizes. Oranges and lemons grow on trees, and strawberries and blackberries grow on bushes.

Blackberries and blueberries grow wild in cooler countries. You can pick them off of bushes, but ask an adult before you do.

Grapes grow on plants called vines. These are grown in long rows that make the grapes easy to pick.

On fruit farms, the plants are looked after as they grow. The fruit is picked by hand or by special machines.

Lunchbox

Add a slice of pineapple to a cheese sandwich for your lunchbox.

Eating fruit

Fruit has **skin** that protects it and makes it easy to carry as a snack. Some fruit has skin that is good to eat, but other fruit has skin that is too tough to chew.

Oranges are covered in a thick skin. Inside are juicy, bite-sized pieces.

Fruits of different colors contain different vitamins and minerals. Eat fruit of all colors to get as many vitamins and minerals as you can.

Vitamin A for healthy skin is found in orange mangoes. A mineral called magnesium for strong bones is found in green kiwi fruit.

Lunchbox

Put pieces of colored fruit on skewers. See how many different colors you can use.

15

Buying and storing

We can buy fresh fruit at a farm store or a supermarket. Fruit with tough skins, such as oranges and lemons, will keep longer than soft fruit, such as peaches and plums.

Fresh fruit is delivered to market stalls in Mexico and Europe every day.

Fruit can be dried in the sunshine or inside a special machine called a **dehydrator**.

Fruit can be frozen, canned, or dried so that it lasts longer. Frozen fruit stored in a freezer lasts for about three months. Canned fruit will last for more than a year.

Lunchbox

Add some dried fruit and slices of banana to your breakfast cereal.

Cooked fruit

Fruit needs to be cooked carefully. If fruit is cooked for too long, it loses some of its goodness and will contain fewer vitamins.

Fruit can be cooked with **savory** food. Here, chicken has been baked with lemon.

Fruit is used to fill pies, tarts, and cobblers. Fresh and dried fruit can be added to muffins and cookies to add flavor.

Lunchbox

Add apples or berries mixed with a little honey to plain yogurt for your lunchbox.

Dried fruit, such as raisins and cherries, is used to make a fruitcake.

Food chart

Here are some examples of foods and drinks that can be made using three types of fruit. Have you tried any of these?

Apple

Apple pie   Apple juice   Dried apple pieces

Orange

Orange juice

Marmalade

Orange cake

Banana

Milkshake

Banana bread

Banana split

A balanced diet

This chart shows you how much you can eat of each food group. The larger the area on the chart, the more of that food group you can eat. For example, you can eat a lot of fruit and vegetables, but only a little oil and sweets. Drink plenty of water every day, too.

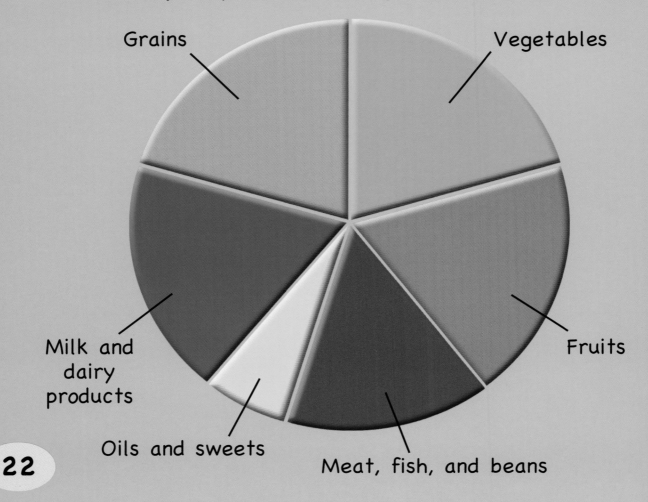

Grains

Vegetables

Milk and dairy products

Fruits

Oils and sweets

Meat, fish, and beans

Our bodies also need exercise to stay healthy. You should spend at least 20 minutes exercising every day, so that your body stays fit and healthy.

Walking to school every day is a great way to exercise.

Glossary

Dehydrator A machine used to dry fruit.

Energy The power we need to live and grow.

Fiber The rough part of fruit. It helps your body to get rid of any unwanted food.

Germs Tiny creatures that can be harmful and can make you sick.

Healthy When you are fit and not sick.

Minerals Important substances that are found in food. Calcium is a mineral that helps to build strong bones.

Orchards Fields of fruit trees.

Ripe Something that is ready to eat.

Savory A food that does not taste sweet.

Seeds Parts of plants that grow to form new plants.

Skin The outside layer of fruit. Oranges have a thick skin called peel. Apples have a thin skin that we can eat.

Vitamins Substances found in food that help our bodies stay healthy.

Index

Web Sites
Due to the changing nature of Internet links, PowerKids Press has developed an online list of Web sites related to the subject of this book. This site is regularly updated. Please use this link to access this list: www.powerkidslinks.com/gfm/fruit